The Twelve Blessings

THE COSMIC CONCEPT

For the New Aquarian Age as given by
The Master Jesus
In His Overshadowing of
George King

REVISED EDITION

The Aetherius Press
LOS ANGELES • FOUNDED 1955 • LONDON

First Published
November, 1958

Second Impression
September, 1959

Third Impression
February, 1961

Fourth Impression
May, 1974

Fifth Impression
March, 1995

Sixth Impression
November, 2000

THE TWELVE BLESSINGS is printed and published by The Aetherius Press,
6202 Afton Place, Hollywood, California 90028-8298, U.S.A.
(323) 465-9652   www.aetherius.org   info@aetherius.org

Printed in The United States of America

The Twelve Blessings were given for the benefit of all humanity through the Everlasting Love of the Cosmic Master — Jesus.

By the same Author:

THE NINE FREEDOMS

CONTACTS WITH THE GODS FROM SPACE

REALIZE YOUR INNER POTENTIAL

YOU TOO CAN HEAL

CONTACT WITH A LORD OF KARMA

OPERATION SPACE POWER

VISIT TO THE LOGOS OF EARTH

YOU ARE RESPONSIBLE!

THE FIVE TEMPLES OF GOD

THE THREE SAVIOURS ARE HERE!

WISDOM OF THE PLANETS

THE PRACTICES OF AETHERIUS

JESUS COMES AGAIN

YOUR HIGHER SELF THROUGH YOGA

FLYING SAUCERS

BOOK OF SACRED PRAYERS

MY CONTACT WITH THE GREAT
    WHITE BROTHERHOOD

A SERIES OF LESSONS IN APPLIED METAPHYSICS

The audio recordings of The Twelve Blessings
    as delivered through Dr. George King by
    the Master Jesus in 1958, are available on
    cassette tape from the publisher.

For more information: **www.aetherius.org**

CONTENTS

PREFACE

ALMOST two thousand years after His resurrection, the Master Jesus returned to deliver His most profound Teachings to our world in the form of The Twelve Blessings. In doing so, He gave the world something even more important than teaching: its greatest religious practice to date.

Over the centuries, Christianity has become distorted by politics, compromise and speculation. The dogmas which underpin so many church denominations today are all too often based on man-made concepts. These were manufactured for reasons of popularity, power or just plain ignorance. Sometimes it was deliberately deceptive, as in the Ecumenical Council decision in 553 A.D., championed by the Emperor Justinian and the Empress Theodora, which declared belief in reincarnation to be a heresy. Sometimes it was well intentioned, as in the attempts by the early Christian Fathers to reconcile different schools of thought within the church by devising the Trinity. But then the road to hell is paved with good intentions, and ultimately the thing which matters above all else in spiritual teaching is whether it is true.

Despite all this, the glorious presence of the Master Jesus has continued to shine on our Earth. The fact that such a beautiful and holy personality existed then and still exists today is a lasting demonstration of the perfection of Divinity. The philosophy He pioneered on Earth has never been bettered: the path of love and service to all life on our world. He lived for it; He died because of it; and He resurrected through it. And now He has opened another chapter in the book of Cosmic Revelation, extending His Sermon on the Mount into the most advanced realms of mystical wisdom by delivering The Twelve Blessings

Originally, The Twelve Blessings were due to be delivered in the year 2010, but the presence on Earth of a great and unique Master, Dr. George King, changed the destiny of human evolution. Trained in advanced yoga techniques, he was able to induce at will the exceptionally rare meditative state known in the east as samadhi. Instead of using this ability to bathe in the unlimited peace and bliss of Divine Oneness, Dr. King used it to become a channel for elevated Masters from this world and beyond, so that they could give Their Teachings to mankind. They were able to transmit Their telepathic communications, known as Transmissions, through his spoken voice. These were recorded on audio tape and the most significant of them were then transcribed and published in printed form. Prominent among these were The Twelve Blessings, delivered between July 27th and October 12th, 1958.

Dr. King was born on January 23rd, 1919, in Shropshire, England. Throughout his childhood, he sought the inner meaning of life, demonstrating healing and psychic powers at an early age. In his early twenties he came into direct contact with the horrors of war, when he served in the Fire Service during the London Blitz, as a conscientious objector. After the war, he devoted himself to the rigorous practice of yoga for eight hours a day for ten years and this while living in London and doing a daytime job. In all my extensive researches over twenty-five years, I have yet to hear of anyone who even claims to have done anything similar to this. His unique combination of single-minded focus and spiritual attainment meant that he could be used by the Masters as Their Primary Terrestrial Mental Channel from his first contact, known as The Command, on May 8th, 1954, until his passing on July 12th, 1997.

There are Transmissions in this publication from four Masters. In order of publication, the first of these is The Master Aetherius, an elevated Being from Venus, Who gave The Command to Dr. King, and Who was a frequent communicator throughout his life. The second is a prominent Master from the Spiritual Hierarchy of this Earth (also known as the Great White Brotherhood), called Saint Goo-Ling. Before each

Blessing, He introduces The Master Jesus, the Venusian Master Who is the third and main source of this spiritual work. And the fourth Master is Mars Sector 6, a Lord of Karma, Who has delivered many other profound Cosmic Teachings through Dr. King.

The Twelve Blessings is a bible for the New Age not just because of the Cosmic Truth it reveals for the first time in our history, but even more for what it represents as a spiritual practice. Never has there been such an advanced system of prayer offered to our world, and yet one which is simple enough for anyone to perform. Its prime purpose is to enable you to help all life in this world and beyond, yet because of its balance it also acts as a perfect method of spiritual development. By sending out energy to the twelve focal points mentioned in the Blessings, by the Law of Karma so must the energy be returned unto you, but in a far more potent way. Hence you build up a cycle of spiritual progress which will transform your life if you practice it regularly.

The Aetherius Society has Headquarters, Branches and Groups all over the world practicing The Twelve Blessings several times a week; pilgrimages are held to Holy Mountains where this holy practice is performed; and thousands of people perform this mystical ritual either regularly or occasionally. Whatever else you decide to include in your spiritual life, I strongly recommend that you make this a part of it. If you do, you will raise your consciousness and become attuned to the highest cosmic levels. More importantly even than this, you will help to improve the Karmic pattern of humanity. The Twelve Blessings enables ordinary people to perform miracles and if ever miracles were needed on our world, they are needed now.

Dr. Richard Lawrence
Executive Secretary, European Headquarters
The Aetherius Society

London, England
November, 2000

8

FOREWORD

THE Aetherius Society has, since its inception, been instrumental in making known the Great Teachings of the Cosmic Masters to the present Aquarian Age.

Now the Society is still further privileged by being chosen as the Organisation through which Jesus, Himself, gave the Sacred Truths known as The Twelve Blessings.

I too feel honoured as the human instrument who was Overshadowed by the Master Jesus, so that He could radiate essential Energies to all men on Earth and also give to them a wide Cosmic Concept in these mystic texts.

When Jesus walked the Earth as a man, He taught the path to God-realisation through Love and Service. At that time His Teachings were given at the beginning of a Cosmic Cycle known as the Piscean Age.

In The Twelve Blessings, Jesus, operating from His own shining Planet, Venus, has again given to Earth great Teachings on the eve of the new Cosmic Cycle—the Aquarian Age.

These Teachings, given as actual Blessings, are an extension of those He gave two thousand years ago. In those days, from the clay of Earth, He gave to the Earth a moral and ethical code of behaviour specially designed to ignite the Flame of Spirituality within man so that he could live successfully within his environment.

The Twelve Blessings constitute a great extension to His previous Teachings inasmuch as they give to thinking, believing man, a tremendously wide conception of the vast Universe and a deeper appreciation of the everlasting Reality of the One Supreme Creative Intelligence behind all manifestation. Here are mighty Cosmic Truths given with a simplicity which is the hallmark of the true understanding found only in the consciousness of a Great Avatar.

The Twelve Blessings have been given so that by their continued study as profound Truths and use as mystic practices, the student may better prepare himself for the journey into the enlightened state of Cosmic Consciousness. The energy released by the student must be returned from the point to which it was directed. The Twelve Blessings, therefore, constitute a system of sacred practices by the continued use of which the student may avail himself of the energy necessary to gain enlightenment. Even more important than this, the student can be energised to that extent which enables him to be of great service to all humanity. It is this type of service through Spiritual enlightenment which the Earth so desperately needs in these dark days. It was to bring about a Spiritual revitalisation of Earth that Jesus released His transmuting Power of pure, selfless Love during these Blessings.

It was to enable those who feel that they must be of service to humanity fully to prepare themselves for such service, that the Great Avatar gave these Twelve Blessings as sacred mystic practices.

Now the disciple is requested to regard the Cross as the symbol of Resurrection, as the symbol of transformation of his apathy into the enlightened state of action through the application of wise ability.

Humanity needs this Power, this Teaching, this Cosmic Love, in order to survive the ordeal of coming painful experiences.

This is the advice given by Jesus, Himself, in these texts, advice which cannot be bettered by anyone.

"Oh adorable little children, take these, My texts—and read them well. Accept them as your Bible—and ACT upon these—and you will be of great service to your brothers."

GEORGE KING.

10

JESUS BLESSES THIS BOOK

Between 12.30 a.m. and 3.30 a.m., on the morning of January 19th, 1959, a happening which will eventually have its effect upon the religious beliefs of this World took place hundreds of miles from Earth in the purple magnificence of star-studded Space. An earth person stood face to face with Jesus and heard Him Bless this Book. Saw Him place it in a beautifully ornate box and take it away with him.

Some days prior to this, Mary King, Mother of George King, was instructed to prepare herself for a physical meeting with Beings from another World. She was at this time directed to . . . *" Bring the Book. This must not be touched by any at Aetherius House, save our Mental Channel."*

She took along a copy of The Twelve Blessings to the rendezvous point, where she was picked up by a Space Craft, Commanded by a Being known as MARS SECTOR 8.

After a wonderful journey, the Space Ship entered a Mother Craft. The Great Master Jesus, Himself, entered, approached the Commander and said:

" Give Me the Book."

The Master Jesus then took It in both hands and this is what He said :

> " Oh, Supreme Master of all Creation,
>
> Higher than the Highest,
>
> Mightier than the Mightiest,
>
> Greater than all Greatness,
>
> We bring to Thee this offering in Love and humility
>
> From our beloved brother of Earth—George,
>
> The one Whom Thou didst choose to be a Leader
>
> Among men of Earth, in this their New Age."

Then after that, He placed the Book in the box and it fitted exactly. Mary King then heard wonderful music fill the whole room and was so affected that she wept aloud. After a few moments of this Cosmic Music, Jesus turned and said as He held the box with the book in it :

> " Blessed is he, who reading this Book doth understand.
>
> But exalted is he, even among the Angels,
>
> Who, reading this Book, doth take it to his heart
>
> And follow its precepts.
>
> Tell my Son, that this Book is now and forever—Holy."

(Full details of this amazing happening appear in Cosmic Voice Issue No. 20.)

HOW TO USE THE TWELVE BLESSINGS

The **Twelve Blessings** can be used either by an individual or by a group. The procedure is the same in either case. The following simple rules will help you greatly.

No. 1. About 15 minutes before The Practice, darken the room, switch on a **green** light. Burn Incense or put a few spots of Tibetan Flower Oils on a piece of cloth and suspend it. Leave the room empty for the vibrations to settle down.

No. 2. Enter the room and breathe slowly and deeply for a few minutes.

No. 3. Request the Violet Flame from the Logos of the Earth to come upwards through the feet and through the Aura to The Heart Center which is situated in the Aura opposite the bottom of the chest bone and a few inches in front of the body.

No. 4. Think down a brilliant white light through the Aura and the brain. Try to feel every molecule of your brain vibrate with this Power. Think it down through the neck, through the shoulders, into the Heart Center.

Begin the Practice of **The Twelve Blessings.**

No. 5. Read out either the whole of The First Blessing or just the chapter heading, i.e. " Blessed Are They Who Work For Peace ".

No. 6. Hold a short silence during which time, visualise a vibrant white light leaving the Heart Center and mentally request that this Light goes to the Group Soul of the Workers for Peace. Hold your hands out in front of you, palms outwards.

No. 7. When you have done this, read out the Prayer at the end of that Blessing.

No. 8. Continue with The Second Blessing followed by a silence, then the Prayer and so on. Always read the **whole** of The Twelfth Blessing, standing as you do so.

No. 9. After you have done this, it is a good thing to perform the Practice of the Presence as given in Rule No. 3. Afterwards visualise a Great Golden Flame which comes from the Golden Sphere over the top of your head, downwards through the whole Aura and physical body.

Special Note :

If a group meet together, get your best reader to read out each Blessing text or chapter heading (depending upon the time you have to devote to this) while the rest of the group should visualise the White Spiritual Light radiating from them.

INTRODUCTION

A T 1.00 a.m. on the morning of July 10th, 1958, the Master Aetherius, Cosmic Adept and Representative of the Planet Venus in the Inter-planetary Parliamentary System, made the following statements as an introduction to the unprecedented importance of the Spiritual Operation known as The Twelve Blessings.

THE MASTER AETHERIUS

"I really have not much to say to you this morning, but what I do say will be of very great importance.

"Regarding The Twelve Blessings. This Operation will be extremely important for Terra as a whole, especially for the country of England.

"There is no reason why you should not know this. It will be very important for England for two reasons. One I may not give to you but the other I may.

"The continuance of England, Scotland and Wales will depend upon several factors, the most important factor being the Energy released during this Operation. As fantastic as this may sound—it is TRUE !

"Even slight appreciation of this fact will give you all some idea of its great importance. It is vital to these Islands, that this Energy be released before the end of the second week in October.

"While this Mental Channel is being used as a Voice by the Master Jesus, great Energies will be radiated. That is why you have been previously requested to man your instrument, so that these Energies could be radiated outwards. (Note 1).

"The people who attend in physical bodies will also have a mild Energy—relatively of course—put through them at the same time. So virtually,

The Twelve Blessings will then be made Twelve very special Transmissions, so that the Energy can be radiated throughout Terra. This Operation, dear friends, is vitally important. Thus do we intend to work to bring about a certain result.

"Because of the vital importance of this Spiritual Operation, it is necessary that Mental Channel Number One is given—and obeys—certain very definite instructions.

"He will observe silence during the previous hours of the days upon which the Blessings will be delivered.

"The diet will be light—at least until after each Transmission.

"The breath will be long during these days.

"If we see it necessary to suspend all other forms of Transmission, in order to relieve strain during this period, we will certainly do so! It really depends upon the co-operation given to this individual by those around him, as to whether a suspension of all other Transmissions is seen to be necessary. I leave that in your hands, so that you may think and discuss this.

"He will continue with the practice he was given some time ago. He will not miss this practice ! (Note 2).

"You may wonder why we are being so definite —why I am now giving orders.

"We request most people—but the Few we order. You should know why these orders are given in this way to this one—who is not quite what he appears to be !

"Now, my dear friends, it was essential that these things went upon record. There will come a time when the Truth will be known to you—and you will be quite amazed—yes, quite amazed ! Yet it is written now in your hearts, if you would but go far enough inwards, bring it outwards and examine it in the light of unbiased

15

reason, you would then know what is written upon the Book of Entry into your system of Birth and Re-birth. You would also know what is written upon the Book of Exit from this wheel of limitation. Then you would know what the Lords of Karma think—and why !

"Certain other instructions will be given when the time is right.

"Now, before I vacate my Transmission Orbit, I will give Terra the benefit of my Invocation.

"**I Invoke the Power**

From the Masters of the Sun and Saturn —
This very moment.
May this Power fall upon your heads—this very moment—
May this Power fall upon your heads—this very moment—
May this Power fall upon your heads—this very moment.
So that, you may know that
God dwells silently within you all."

"Good morning, my dear friends.

"May God bless each and every one of you sweet ones here."

NOTE 1.

Reference is made here to a specially constructed piece of radionic apparatus which acted as a radiator for subtle Pranic Energies. The basic principle underlying its operation was that of a "safety valve." This apparatus radiated the Energy released during The Twelve Blessings so as to avoid a state of energetic saturation, which would have damped down the flow of Energy as it was released through George King and all those present.

NOTE 2.

This practice, although simple, had deep metaphysical implications.

The First Blessing

SAINT GOO-LING

"THESE Blessings will be of very great importance to your Earth, especially to this part of it. The One you knew as Jesus will release great Energy to this country in which you now reside.

"I would ask the organisers to obtain a little Cross for all those present, so that these little Crosses may be Blessed by Jesus on the Twelfth Time. These little Crosses must not be worn but must be kept in your secret and Holy Place, so that you all might re-charge yourselves when the Karma Yoga does sap your strength.

"This will be done.

"You will then—after the Twelfth Time—go out into the World and if your hearts be pure, you will spread much Love and some Wisdom—for you will know many things 'twixt now and then.

"I go!"

BLESSED ARE THEY WHO WORK FOR PEACE

THE MASTER JESUS

"Oh my adorable children, I pray that the very Light of God doth shine upon you now, so that your hearts may be filled with this Power. So that your minds may be filled with this Wisdom, which floweth from the very Heart of Great and Mighty God like a river which knoweth no dam.

17

"BLESSED ARE THEY WHO WORK FOR PEACE.

"In these times of unrest in your World, the workers for Peace are indeed thrice Blessed. For these Ones, by their toil, sacrifice their own bliss.

"By their interest in the suffering of their brothers they sacrifice their peace.

"Blessed are these Ones at this time.

"Their handiworks will increase and their monuments, built upon sure foundations, will last so that the future generations may look in reverence upon these.

"Thrice Blessed in the NOW—and by NOW— are these Ones, for they have demonstrated unselfishness in the most definite and Holy way.

"This strange World needs the guiding hands of these Ones and they give their hands to the strangers in the wilderness of materialism.

"They light the beacons in the darkness.

"They open the oasis in the desert.

"They are the backbone of modern civilisation.

"Thrice Blessed are these Ones.

"Oh workers, who in unselfish sacrifice, share the burden with your brothers, I say unto you, that even though the way be rough and long and dark, you will be helped and guided in your passage, so that you may guide and help those stumbling ones who see not the Light—in the midst of Light. Who feel not the warmth of the Heart of God. Who hear not the voice of their real Selves.

"You help these—and you will be great, even though you seek not praise.

"Oh Mighty Father of all Creation,
Let Your Light
Flow through this World—NOW.
Let it shine into the hearts and minds of men now,
So that all may look within and see the
Glory of Thine Everlasting Being.
Oh Spirit of Spirits,
Let Your Love
Flow through the hearts and minds of man—NOW.
So that he may look within and see the
Great and Wondrous Glory
Of his Divine heritage."

"SO ENDETH THE FIRST BLESSING.

"Adorable children—GO WITH GOD."

—Delivered on Sunday, July 27th, 1958.

The Second Blessing

SAINT GOO-LING

"IF you go within you can contact the Source of All Things. Then must you come out again and give the fruits from the Garden of Wisdom to your hungry brothers.

"I go!"

BLESSED ARE THE WISE ONES

THE MASTER JESUS

"Oh my adorable children, may your hearts and minds be filled with Love and Wisdom, so that you may radiate this Light of God throughout your Earth.

"BLESSED ARE THE WISE ONES, FOR THEY WALK THROUGH A DARK AND IGNORANT WORLD, SPREADING THEIR LIGHT.

"So that all who want to—so that all who are ready—may see—even though blindly—some facet of the Face of God. Some small part of His Work.

"Thrice Blessed are these Wise Ones.

"These are the Ones who have gone within— deep within—and made a glorious and lasting contact with the Spark which dwelleth there. The self-same Spark, which came from the Heart of the Mighty Logos. From the Heart of He—and It—which fashioned even the Logos.

"Thrice Blessed are the Wise Ones, in the NOW —and by NOW.

" Yet what Bliss they sacrifice for man.

" These Ones have found Peace and have turned away from it, to give its very essence, its very core, to searching, groping, un-peaceful man.

" These are Great Ones. Without these, this World could not endure.

" Thrice Blessed are the searchers, who have found and left and given of their very heart to man, so that he may See—and Seeing Know—and Knowing ACT—and Acting Become—THAT which he should be.

" SO ENDETH THE SECOND BLESSING.

" Oh adorable children—children of God—walk bravely forward to your Salvation. Look neither to one side nor the other but straight ahead into the very Face of God and contact this Mighty Light, so that It may shine upon you. So that It may impregnate you forever.

" Be this NOW—by NOW.

" Adorable ones, little children, I am here with you. I will lead you into this state, if you will but hold out your hand to me.

" Adorable ones—GO WITH GOD."

—Delivered on Sunday, August 3rd, 1958.

The Third Blessing

"THE Energy which will be released during these Blessings, will be of great benefit to this country. What will be said, will be of great importance but not so important as the Energy called LOVE which will be released during these sayings.

" Try to sit still and lose yourselves in the great sea of White Light which will flow through you all, out into your country and to the World as a whole.

" Try to be so detached from surroundings, that you can be a worth-while instrument in this metaphysical and highly Spiritual Operation.

" If you do this to the best of your ability, you will advance very much, even though this is not your motive. In fact—I would say not to have this as a motive.

" Be still—and wait.

" I go ! "

BLESSED ARE THEY WHO LOVE

THE MASTER JESUS

" Oh adorable children, may your hearts be filled with the simple Love of Wondrous God. May your minds be filled with the Wisdom of this only Source, so that you may all realise your Divine heritage.

" BLESSED ARE THEY WHO LOVE, FOR THEY ARE THE DISCIPLES OF GOD.

" These Ones, often in great pain and anguish themselves, think naught of this but do transmute the very forces of Holy Nature into this Mighty Energy called Love, so that they may give it freely to those who need it.

" Thrice Blessed are these Ones, in the NOW—and by NOW.

" Theirs is the difficult task of transmutation of the base energies into that state of Energy you call LOVE.

" These Ones possess naught—for they have given it ALL to their brothers.

" They can love not themselves, for they have given the very seed of their hearts to those whose hearts are empty. Whose hearts yearn to be filled.

" They can think naught of their own Salvation, for even this, these great Ones, these Holy Ones, these Everlasting Ones, have cast at the feet of God.

" They have taken from their bowed heads their Crowns of Triumph, their Crowns of Achievement and cast these in Holy sacrifice at the root of the Throne of their own Salvation.

" Thrice Blessed—aye and seven times Blessed —and seven again—are these Ones, for such sacrifice as this can only come from the hearts of the Cosmic Lovers.

" They love not any man—because they love ALL.

" These are Blessed.

" These are the Ones who will save the pitiful ones, for these are they who will become the very essence of the heartbeats of the pitiful ones, for they will be instrumental in helping greatly to transmute the only devil which exists upon this Earth.

" The Lovers of God, through man, will be the

Ones who will light a Light in the hearts of all men, so that Wisdom may enter into these vessels so purified.

"Thrice Blessed are these Ones. Aye—and seven times seven times seven, Blessed are they.

"SO ENDETH THE THIRD BLESSING.

"Oh adorable children, be at Peace. Let the Light of God flow through your hearts and minds —and you *will* be at Peace.

"Let not ugly ambition raise its greedy head before you, whispering terrible promise into your brain.

"Let not the four-headed monster—possession —breathe its hot breath upon your hearts but— *be at Peace.*

"Walk ye into Peace. Request it gently, for it falleth even as the gentle rain from Heaven. Let it flow. Offer to this wondrous Power no resistance—but let it flow through you all—NOW.

"Every cell of your body will rejoice. Every part of you will be happy 'neath this Light.

"For, dear friends—adorable children—*first cometh the Angel, Peace—to make way for the Goddess—LOVE.*

"Open up the door, let Peace enter in, then will come the Other in splendour, to live forever within your soul.

> "**Oh Mighty God,**
> **Who is the Creator of All Things,**
> **We pray that Your Light**
> **May shine through us all,**
> **So that we may transmit this unto the World.**"

"Oh My children—GO WITH GOD."

—Delivered on Sunday, August 10th, 1958.

The Fourth Blessing

SAINT GOO-LING

"DURING these Blessings much Power will be radiated outwards to all. The actual people who are chosen as the recipients of these Blessings are not chosen so much in order of importance but with a more important reason underlying the position of choice.

"Sometimes, now, one part needs some Power, sometimes in future another part needs Power. Such knowledge as this has given the sequence to the choice.

"It should be made known at this time, that the great Love and Power of Jesus is just as much alive today on this Earth, as ever it was.

"A short time ago the man you see before you went out to the top of a mountain in order to pray for Peace. The Mighty Jesus Himself, came and stood at his right hand. He pointed the sceptre of Power towards this Adept. The Adept then manipulated these Energies so that a war could be avoided. The next day—and afterwards—the war fizzled out, in what was, to Earth man the most mysterious manner.*

"We do not expect the ordinary man to be able to perform feats which are the capabilities of the extra-ordinary man but we would remind the ordinary man, that he can perform feats which are even above his imagination, if only he will co-operate in very active way with one of the Cosmic Adepts, who are now very active on and around Earth.

*(See *Cosmic Voice*, Issue No. 18, pages 10-17 inc.).

" You all can play your part and so help the great forces of Light to transmute the forces of darkness in your Earth but you must be prepared to leave the comfort of your homes in order to do this. No Initiate became an Initiate because he liked comfort.

" And this is so—and will always be so !

" I go ! "

BLESSED ARE THE PLANETARY ONES

THE MASTER JESUS

" Oh adorable children, may your hearts and minds be filled with the Wondrous Love and Light of Mighty God, so that—you may see within some dim reflection of your true Being. For you can become veritable Gods if you would but reach outwards and grasp this heritage but reach inwards and become at Peace with your Higher Self.

" BLESSED ARE THE PLANETARY ONES WHO HAVE, AT THIS TIME, SACRIFICED PEACE, SACRIFICED FRIENDSHIP, SACRI-FICED THEIR VERY SALVATION FOR YOU.

" Thrice Blessed are these Ones.

" They have answered the call of the Great Ones and without a moment's hesitation, they have left their Planetary bliss to accept terrible limitation among you, so that your passage through experience may be guaranteed.

" These are the Ones who have left their homes —their Spiritual homes—who have left their brothers—their Spiritual brothers—in order to watch over you. These are the Ones, who, day by day, suffer the unspeakable hell of terrible alone-ness, in order to give you their hearts. These are the Ones who suffer, day by day, in a thousand psychological ways, so that—the dark

26

little Earth may make its revolutions through Evolution.

" There are no words to describe the suffering or the depth of sacrifice of these Ones.

" Thrice Blessed are these—at this moment throughout all Earth.

" I ask you to remember these Ones in your every prayer, for by their sacrifice you can gain wonderful experience and this the greatest gift from man—or even God—to man.

" They walk, unsung, in silence through a dark World. They tarry here and the Light doth come. And then they pass onwards before the takers of that Light do realise what has happened to them.

" They take upon themselves terrible Karma, awful responsibility, do these Ones and yet, they murmur not.

" In the name of God, these Wondrous Beings are now Blessed.

" When the record is written up by the hand of Truth, indeed will these Ones be classed among the greatest in all the System.

" SO ENDETH THE FOURTH BLESSING.

" Oh sweet little children, let your minds and hearts be open to the gentle Power which floweth like a deep river from the Heart of God. It floweth into your Spirit—from there it illuminates the Soul. Let it come outwards, into your mind and heart, from the Soul of you. Let it flow gently, in sweet Peace, so that you might be illuminated by this everlasting stream, which is the Love of God for the lower Aspects of God.

" My children, learn stillness of body. Move ye not. Learn stillness of heart. Let not the Lake of Peace be ruffled by violent emotion. Learn stillness of mind, for Peace will not come while you move like restless animals.

" Oh Divine and Everlasting Spirit,
We pray that Your Mighty Power
May fall upon the World—NOW.
We pray that this might enter into all men,
So that they may have some small
Glimpse of themselves and that this
Glimpse—even though but dimly seen—
Might be forever a monument at the
Crossroads of their inspiration."

" My children—GO WITH GOD."

—*Delivered on Sunday, August 17th, 1958.*

The Fifth Blessing

"IN these days few men on this World ever give thanks to the Devic Realms for Their tireless work on behalf of backward mankind.

"Those who do this are remembered by the Gods.

"I go !"

BLESSED ARE THE THANKSGIVERS

THE MASTER JESUS

"Oh sweet and most wonderful children, you are now being filled with the Power and Love of Holy God.

"BLESSED ARE THE THANKSGIVERS, FOR THEY TURN GREAT TIDES OF ENERGY AND DIRECT THESE TOWARDS THEIR OBJECTIVES.

"Blessed are they who have expended enough energy themselves so that they may know of the existence of the Devic Kingdom and knowing this, live in eternal thanks for Its work.

"Blessed are these Ones.

"They walk in lonely silence upon the shores of many seas, sending out beams of their Love to Mighty Neptune and His Hosts.

"They labour in a thousand fields and oft' times give thanks unto those who protect the fertility of their seed.

"They walk through a thousand woods sending out rays of thought from their minds to those who dwell in man's invisibility, therein.

"I say unto you now, that these Ones are indeed Thrice Blessed, for they demonstrate their belief and Love of God in a most practical way. It dawns upon these Ones what debt they owe to the Devic Helpers.

"These are the Ones who pay their Spiritual debt to those who sacrifice in order to render to them great service, which results in a definite road through experience.

"Thrice Blessed are they who send their Power and Love to the Devas.

"Who walk in the rain with bared heads and Bless those who shake the clouds. Who stand in flood and Bless those who have sent it.

"Ordinary Earth man by his wrong thought and action has for countless centuries sent streams of Power to the Devas, Power discoloured by his uncontrolled emotion. The Devas, having no other tools but those of man, have had to make flood and drought. Man is responsible for all these—and all these will be reckoned in his Karma.

"Thrice Blessed are they who provide the Devas with the Spiritual tools, so that—They may build Their empires upon the rock of balance.

"Oh children of Earth, walk ye into the night and thank your God for it. Walk ye into the dawn and thank your God for it. Walk ye into the sunset and thank your God for it and you will be helping the Silent Workers to preserve balance for you.

"Thrice Blessed are those who have done this —and this is NOW—by NOW.

"SO ENDETH THE FIFTH BLESSING.

" Oh Divine Spirit of Everlasting Life,
Let the Mighty Power of Thy Love
Flow forth into all the peoples of the World,
So that they may be risen up to realise their Divinity.
So that they may live and act in this Light ;
To let this Light flow forth forever through them.
Oh Mighty God—there will be no barriers now ! "

" Adorable children—GO WITH GOD."

—Delivered on Sunday, August 24th, 1958.

The Sixth Blessing

SAINT GOO-LING

"BEFORE these Blessings, all those who come along should sit in silence. During this silence you should all think through your physical and mental bodies the Transmuting Power of the Velvet Fire. For that is really how it feels, just like soft velvet when it caresses your aura, with its Violet fingers. You should then think upwards this Flame of Transmutation and then your bodies will be clean.

"This is the finest practice for all students of Truth in these days. If you could place around yourselves a protecting wall of this Velvet Flame, you would be absolutely invulnerable from all types of attack by the dark forces. There are unique exceptions to this rule but these do not apply to you people.

"Think then, this Violet coloured Velvet Flame up through your aura and your body and make out of it a huge protective shell in which you can live in cleanliness and also continue with your Spiritual work.

"This practice has been given to you by Master Aetherius. So great was His love that He saw fit to reveal it so that all men may use this Spiritual Practice.

"In future, all of you will do this before the next Blessing and after the Blessing you can then think down the Great and Mighty Golden Fire from the Spark within and let this Golden Fire give Wisdom to your brain, Love to your

Heart and understanding which is lodged in the Solar Plexus Centre. All these things you can do. If you do these things, great change will be brought about within you.

"You noticed, even this very night, that your Earth Leader allowed himself only two and a half minutes in which to gain rapport with me. All the manipulations necessary to heighten one part of consciousness and dampen another, could be done easily in this time.

"This should be an illustration to all, that if you use Great Power of Violet Flame properly, you can raise your consciousness and also do much good to your body and your mind and your emotions and your etheric and your soul. Practice many times and one day perfection—like a Sun—will dawn. Then will you rejoice, for you will have found the Great Secret. Treat this in a Sacred manner, for it is very great, most Holy Practice.

"I go ! "

BLESSED ARE THEY WHO HEAL

THE MASTER JESUS

"Oh sweet little children, I give you My Heart. I give you all the absolute benefit of My Love. Oh sweet ones, know that by your thought and action of today you carve—tomorrow. Live always, dear adorable children, within the Light which shineth from the Divine Spark within you all.

"Make your brain live in everlasting thankfulness for experience. Make your heart live in everlasting praise for your Divinity and then—as sure as God—you will *be* a veritable God.

"BLESSED ARE THEY WHO HEAL IN THESE DAYS OF GREAT PAIN AND SUFFERING.

33

" Oft' times these Ones sacrifice their own Peace so that—others may benefit.

" Thrice Blessed are these Ones, for this Holy Sacrifice.

" I say unto you, man—he who in total disregard of universal suffering does search in these days for Peace, will find it not. For alas, ye are commanded even now, as ye were yesterday, to spread yourselves in sacrificial action throughout your suffering World.

" Thrice Blessed are those who do this, are those who work for no reward in this Earth, in order to bring some Peace of mind to those who suffer.

" Blessed are the Ones who lay their hands upon the fevered brow of their brothers, knowing that their request will be answered. Knowing that Great Power will flow through them, like water through a river course.

" Blessed are these Ones, for they are living their belief.

" It is indeed wrong of the so-called Christian Church to turn the deaf ears of dogmatic limitation upon the feats of these Ones. For these are the Ones who will be instrumental in bringing the Light of Practice again into the Christian Church. Even though some of them regard themselves not as Christians, yet, by their very action they demonstrate more Christianity in one Healing pass than their devout brothers do in all their surface prayers.

" I AM JESUS, WHO STEPPED UPON THIS WORLD TO BRING THE WAY TO GOD THROUGH LOVE AND SERVICE.

" I now Bless those who give service to Me, to their brothers and to God in this way.

" Thrice Blessed are the Healers, for they will

34

bring Light into My Church.

"For they are the Ones, who, when the time is ripe, will LEAD My Church.

"SO ENDETH THE SIXTH BLESSING.

" Oh Divine Lord of all Wondrous Creation,
We raise our voices and minds to You—NOW—in prayer.
Knowing even as we do, that this is answered at this
moment.
Oh Wondrous God,
We ask that the hearts and minds of man
Might be opened to Thy Presence,
To Thy Mighty Light.
So that they may forever Glorify Thee.
So that they may realise, that within them
Beats a Spark directly connected to
Thy Wondrous Heart.
We raise our minds in thankfulness
For the fulfilment of our prayer,
For this SHALL—come to pass
Upon this Earth."

"Oh adorable children, you have been instructed—go ye forth and obey.

"Go ye forth with your hand in the soft Violet hand of the Sacred Transmuting Power of God.

"Oh, sweet ones—GO WITH GOD."

—Delivered on Sunday, August 31st, 1958.

The Seventh Blessing

SAINT GOO-LING

"THE Blessing today will be very important, in view of the vandalism of men, who defy the basic Laws of Metaphysics by their devastating journey into the perfection of the tiny Universe—the Atom.

"As a result of this, much of a part of your country lies beneath water. Had it not been for the Energy released by these Blessings up to now, most of your fertile country would be flooded.

"There will come a day when the vandals will have to swallow this bitter pill, for it is written that the mills grind slowly—but with great surety.

"This is the Law of Inevitability—which is a descriptive name for KARMA.

"Pay attention all—with your hearts.

"Be quiet all—and listen to the Mighty Blessing.

"I go !"

BLESSED IS THE MOTHER EARTH

THE MASTER JESUS

"My sweet adorable children, you come again to make some contact with your God.

"Oh sweet adorable ones, it is written that if you knock loud and often enough upon the door which leads to complete and absolute Realisation of the Existence and Unchangable Reality of God, then must this portal be opened unto you.

"Knock, Oh seekers, with the hands of your Faith and into those hands will be placed the key to the door of Reality.

"BLESSED IS THE MOTHER EARTH.

"Blessed is She, Who, in sacrifice, has made a Space Refuge for you all.

"Blessed is She, Who, instead of taking the unlimited gowns allowed to this Goddess, did accept material limitation, so that you—the lower Aspects of God—could walk through experience back to God again.

"Blessed is the Logos of this Earth, for She shineth like a Sun doth shine. Yet—of purpose— She hideth this Light beneath the bushel of a material form, which renders unto man, sustenance.

"Blessed is the Logos of this Earth.

"She weeps not when the vandals do tear Her body with wounds. She weeps not when the fools do commit foul acts against the very Nature, which forms Her Fruits.

"As yet, man, She has borne you.

"I request most strongly NOW—that you do not take such for granted.

"She has not, as yet, demanded that you change—or leave.

"Thrice Blessed is such a One as this. For by Her Wondrous selfless actions, She proves how near unto Her Source, She really be.

"Thrice Blessed upon all of Her hundred stages is She.

"Seven times Blessed upon all of Her forty-nine cloaks is She, for She has illustrated the great Love —that of sacrificing Salvation for another.

"Her Mighty Flame now burns within Her large Heart.

" There was a time when the whole of the Galactic System could see this but alas, ye have quenched it.

" Thrice Blessed, by God Thrice Blessed is She, Who has endured such terrible limitation upon your behalf. And yet, when Her seeking children come together and ask for the Violet Flame of Transmutation, She gives this willingly. She gives this always, asking nothing in return for Her sacrifice.

" You are *commanded* to think of these things and spread them like seeds of Truth, abroad. Then, dear friends, you will be helping the Great One in the limitation She has accepted on your behalf.

" Thrice Blessed is the Wondrous Logos of this Earth.

" In the NOW—and by NOW.

" SO ENDETH THE SEVENTH BLESSING.

" Oh my adorable children, seek within, find Peace and then leave it. And then give it to those who have not found it—and you will be great, for you will be suffering so that others may pick the fruits of Wisdom. *This is the true measure of the greatness of either man or God.*

" Man dwelleth in a world of selfishness—God dwelleth in a world of selfless expansion.

" Bridge this gap—and be a GOD.

> **" Oh Mighty Creator,**
> **Let the Wondrous beams of Your Majestic Power**
> **Flow through all the children upon the Earth—**
> **this very moment.**
> **So that they may reach upwards and realise**
> **The Divinity of their heritage."**

" Adorable children—GO WITH GOD."

—*Delivered on Sunday, September 7th, 1958.*

The Eighth Blessing

SAINT GOO-LING

"THIS Blessing will be the most important one to date—so would request that you all sit still and absorb the Power released by this Mighty Blessing and send it to the Focal Point, as depicted in this Blessing. You will be doing very great service to your Earth if you do this, as you will see very shortly.

" It is a certain fact that if a man builds up a path through the ether and sends upon this path his Love and Blessings towards Master he receives great Power which is sent back along the same path as that he used in the first place.

" This is a metaphysical fact and can be proven beyond all doubt to he who is willing to give up time and energy to this practice. Such a one is indeed forging the strong foundations of a bridge for himself that he may use this to cross into the Realms of Light.

" Now be still !

" Around you all is a very great wall of protection. Even so, such is the foul action of mankind that he has brought much contamination to all layers of atmosphere and also to the ether which contains this—that Cosmic Communication is very difficult at this time.

" So please send out Power to the Focal Point, which will be given in this Blessing.

" I go ! "

BLESSED IS THE MIGHTY SUN

THE MASTER JESUS

" Oh My sweet adorable children, once again you come as a practical demonstration of your Faith in God.

" This do I say unto you, Oh sweet ones, you will not find this Faith an empty thing—but filled with Light which will impregnate your heart and soul, so that you will be prepared to pay a visit to the God within.

" I say to you—have not Faith for the sake of Faith—*but have Faith for God's sake—and your own* !

" BLESSED IS THE MIGHTY SUN.

" Blessed is the Solar Logos, for upon this you and I depend for that vital Energy which doth take us through valuable experience.

" Blessed is this One, for It shineth always in complete sacrifice upon the behalf of ye—and Me —and all of us who dwell within Its House.

" Send out your Love to This. Send out your Power to This. Know that even as you do so, never in a thousand million years can you hope to repay the debt you owe to this most Wondrous Being—this most magnificently glorious Aspect of Great God.

" Oh men of Earth, turn thy face towards the greatest living Entity in thy System and absorb Its Wondrous Power deep into thine Eye, so that, thine heart may be burned clean of impurity—so that thine Eye might dwell upon this Glory. Yet not for dwelling's sake—purely—but more for the sake of thy brother, who is blind through this part.

" Blessed is the Mighty Logos of the Great Sun.

" Even I stand back in awe, when I this pronouncement do make, for indeed here stands a Sacred Jewel in the Heart of God—Itself . . . . .

" Thrice Blessed is this Mighty Logos.

" Seven times Blessed is each one of Its children.

" Seven times Blessed is each one of Its nine thousand dimensions.

" Seven times Blessed is each one of Its nine million, four hundred and fifty-six thousand, nine hundred and twenty-one cloaks.

" Eight times eight times eight times eight times eight times Blessed is the Heart of This.

" And nine times Blessed is the Body of This,

" And twice Blessed in THAT—BY THAT—AS THAT—is the Soul of This.

" And once Blessed in the Heart of God, is the Spirit of This.

" SO ENDETH THE EIGHTH BLESSING.

" If you, my children, would change from men to God-men, you would send your Love always towards this Great Being, which you now take for granted.

" For this is the God of your Bible, it is the Brahma of the Hindu scripts.

" This is the nearest thing to God in *your* concept of manifestation.

" Mark well, Oh children, these words. You will see them written again in the Book of Records— but wait ye not until then — for present action must be your guide.

" Oh adorable children—GO WITH GOD."

—Delivered on Sunday, September 14th, 1958.

The Ninth Blessing

SAINT GOO-LING

"TODAY, Prasad will be distributed afterwards. Those who take this must consume it all. This will now be charged for your benefit. This, as a symbol, is sacrificed to Brahma. (Here the Prasad was Blessed, first a single packet, then the remainder.)

"All those here may take a piece as they leave. Eat it with care—and all of it—for it has been sacrificed to Brahma.

"Now the Blessing today will be of even greater importance—in one way—than the Blessing of last time, for reasons that you will see for yourselves.

"Sit still and be silent, even in your breathing, while this Blessing is given and direct the Power running through you to the Focal Point which will be traced out for you by the Master you knew as Jesus.

"I go ! "

BLESSED ARE THE SUPREME LORDS OF KARMA

THE MASTER JESUS

"Oh my sweet adorable children, you come again to be bathed in the Wondrous Light of Mighty God and you shall be thus impregnated with this Wondrous Force, which cometh in soft gentleness from the Divine Heart.

"Let your Love flow forth, Oh children, unto

those I speak of, for They are Sacred ones—and this Love will be returned, after a little time and it will be fashioned by a greater Love.

" BLESSED ARE THE SUPREME LORDS OF KARMA.

" For these Ones, great above words, more Holy even than the Mighty Sun, stretch Their influence throughout all the Galaxy, so that the Great Laws of God—the Great Laws which ARE GOD—may be perfect in Their balance.

" These Great and Mighty Lords of Karma, make it possible for fools like ye and Me to gain that experience which will lead us to the Godhead —as Conscious Gods.

" Blessed are these Great and Mighty Ones, Who, in millions of time-units, sacrifice Their bliss, so that countless trillions of life-streams, throughout the great Galactic System, may go back to God.

" Blessed are these Ones, in Their Goodness, in Their Justice, in Their Perfection.

" So Holy, so Sacred are these Mighty Beings, that common man may not even know Their Names.

" So Sacred, so Great are these Mighty Beings, that even the Perfects of Saturn, whisper Their Names but gently with a heart full of fashioned respect.

" Men, you will never repay the debt you owe to These Ones.

" Thrice Blessed are the Seven.

" Thrice Blessed are the Fourteen.

" Thrice Blessed are the Twenty-one.

" And once Blessed is the One who stands in the exact Centre of this Circle.

" SO ENDETH THE NINTH BLESSING.

" Oh sweet little God-respecting children, think on these things—but always.

" Do not let a moon set or a Sun set before you think upon them, before you help constructively these Mighty Ones, by the strict control of your own thoughts and actions. Bring these within the Great Law and you will be praying a greater prayer, than that of words.

" Be good, be tolerant, be kind, be merciful, be gentle, be humble and you will be great. Then you will be helping the Sacred Ones Whose Names may not be mentioned—even in closed session.

" Bless your brothers. Bless the Logos of your Earth. Bless the Mighty Solar Logos and then Bless the Supreme Lords of Karma and you will discover a satisfaction beyond all words.

" ACT—in My Name in this way and the reaction will be *Peace* and even something more —something greater than that.

" Oh adorable children—GO WITH GOD."

—Delivered on Sunday, September 21st, 1958.

The Tenth Blessing

"PRASAD will be given to those who come here. Afterwards take this Prasad and eat it all in sacrifice to Brahma. (The Prasad was Blessed.)

" Now today the Blessing of Jesus will be even more important than those others to date—in one way. Be prepared to send your Love to the Being as spoken of by this One.

" The Power will be considerable and would ask those, who are unable for any reason at all to take so much Power as that which will be released this day, to retreat into the upper room. Sit down there quietly and bathe head and neck with cold water.

" Only a fraction of Power, of course, will be directed to any one present but this fraction will be considerable in potency. Do not disturb by making sounds with the cough but retire, because this Blessing is very important. If you do retire of course during this time, you will still be able to get your Charged Cross on the Twelfth Blessing.

" I go ! "

BLESSED IS THE GALAXY

THE MASTER JESUS

" Oh My adorable children, it is written that when a few are gathered together in the Name of My Spirit, there will I be.

" Oh sweet Ones, I take each and every one of you to My Heart, for you come in belief, in knowledge of the existence of Wondrous God. You will be rewarded for your journey.

45

"BLESSED IS THE GREAT BEING KNOWN AS THE GALAXY.

" For this Mighty One, Great in proportion and wondrous in content, stretches through Space Its magnetic Body, so that thousands of inhabited Worlds may reside therein.

" Blessed is this Mighty Lord, for It is One of the Greater Lords of Creation, which is now sacrificing Its Wondrous Self upon the plane of preservation, so that trillions of life-streams may gain essential experience. So that thousands of inhabited Worlds may gain experience. So that great and mighty Suns may gain experience. So that Solar Systems may gain experience.

" What description is there for this ? None— not even in the great language of TUL. . . . . . .

" Blessed is the wondrous Being known as the Galaxy.

" A hundred million aeons ago this wondrous and Mighty Lord did cast Its Crown from Its Head and did sacrifice Itself upon the plane of preservation in order to be of service to the GOD of Gods !

" Thrice Blessed is this Wondrous Being in the NOW—and by NOW.

" Twice times Blessed is the Great and Mighty Central Sun of this Wondrous One.

" And once Blessed as THAT by THAT—in THAT is the Soul within the Centre.

" And always Blessed within the Mind of the ABSOLUTE, is the Spirit of this One within the most Central Position of all.

" Where the very Gods do talk—listens this One.

" Where the very Gods do walk—rides this One.

" Where the very Gods are transmuted—resides this One.

" Thrice Blessed is—IT.

46

"Seven times Blessed are Its children within Its Mighty Globe.

"SO ENDETH THE TENTH BLESSING.

"Oh adorable children, let the God-given Love from your hearts flow out to this Wondrous Being, beyond the mere descriptions of poor, foolish, limited beings like you and I. Realise—at this very moment—the existence of this One and your existence within Its Wondrous Body and thank your God for this existence. For this great and mighty opportunity to travel within such a wondrous Vehicle as this, back to your Source within the Centre of the Godhead.

"This is prayer—prayer beyond the mere babbling of foolish man for possession. For this prayer can only come from the very heart, from the very soul, from the very Centre of your Spirit. Let it flow in the wondrous unchanged Light that it is, to the Source of this Great Being and I say unto you, no matter what your religion or belief, this will be the greatest part of it. This will be the greatest prayer you can offer—up to now.

"Oh Divine One, Who allows us within Thy Body,
Take from our hearts our Love
Into Thine Own Self—this very moment.
We make this sacrifice for we dimly realise
Thy Greatness.
Oh Mighty Jehovah, Lord of Creation,
Compassionate Master of all Life,
Controller of Manifestation,
To Thee we offer our prayer of
Everlasting thankfulness, for the sacrifice
Continually made by Thy Wondrous Angel.
Preserve this One for Its allotted time.
Then, Oh Jehovah, Lord of Lords,
Transmute it into the
Centre of Centres within Thy Mind."

"Oh adorable children—GO WITH GOD."

TAKE GREAT HEED

" This is Mars Sector 6, reporting from Satellite No. 3, now in Magnetisation Orbit of Terra, during Magnetisation Period No. 2. Subject:— TAKE GREAT HEED !

" Oh brothers of Earth, you have just lived through the greatest experience of your countless incarnations upon this Planet—Terra. You have never—not one of you—had an experience comparable with this before. Take this deep into your very heart, into your very soul, into your very Spirit—and learn by it.

" Indeed is the Great and Mighty Galaxy a wondrous, shining Being — which defies the description of even the Lord of the Sun.

" Better than you, do we realise this, for millions of years in your time we have patrolled the Body of this gigantic God.

" It lives, It breathes, It thinks, It feels pain, It meditates, in the same way as does the Logos of a Planet. Yet within Its Great and Mighty Structure there are thousands upon thousands of inhabited Worlds, hundreds of Mighty Suns, dozens of Great and Mighty Invisible Suns and the One Central Sun.

" Yet It is a Being.

" Fantastic indeed is Truth !

" Take what you have heard, Oh brothers of Terra, into yourselves and pray for the existence of this Great and Mighty One ; because your debt will never be paid—save by Divine cancellation— to this One.

" This is Mars Sector 6, reporting from Satellite No. 3. Now in Magnetisation Orbit—Terra.

48

SPECIAL ANNOUNCEMENT.

" Since this Blessing by the Cosmic Master from Venus you knew as Jesus, the Spiritual Aspect of the Power Absorption Factor has risen to 49. The physical Aspect has risen to 10.*

" Do you see, Oh brothers, better, what I meant when I stated that this has been your greatest experience ?

" Forget it not. Live with it and let it live with you. For the morrow can even bring a greater dawn.

" This Transmission came from Mars Sector 6, from Satellite No. 3—now in Magnetisation Orbit of Terra. Through Primary Terrestrial Mental Channel. With the Sanction and Authority of Interplanetary Parliament, based upon the Planet Saturn.

" WITH THE SANCTION AND AUTHORITY OF THE SUPREME LORDS OF KARMA.

" WITH THE SANCTION AND AUTHORITY OF THE ADEPTS FROM THE CENTRE.

" LIVE — REMEMBER — REALISE.

" All Transmissions now discontinued."

—*Delivered on Sunday, September 28th, 1958.*

*See *The Nine Freedoms* (published by The Aetherius Society) pages 85-92 for an explanation of the activities of Satellite No. 3.

The Eleventh Blessing

"NOW, again Prasad will be offered to all. Afterwards take Prasad and eat all in sacrifice to Brahma. (The Prasad was Blessed.)

"Now, Blessing this time even greater than before. Please send out all your Love to those Great and Mighty Beings, who will be mentioned in this Blessing.

"By doing this you will be performing very Holy Prayer and also by the Great Law you must attract that Energy again, down to your Earth. Then will you be instrumental directly in helping your Earth in this way.

"You will also be helping the Cosmic Masters who have—in most ways—to *work through Earth man,* in order to impregnate the Earth with Their Powers.

"Focus your attention as directed and let your Love flow forth.

"I go ! "

BLESSED ARE THE SUPREME LORDS OF CREATION

THE MASTER JESUS

"Oh adorable little children, I take you to My heart—NOW—saying unto you, that your Faith shall be rewarded, even at the time when you least expect this. For you dwelleth within My Embrace, when you meet for service in My Name.

50

"BLESSED ARE THE SUPREME LORDS OF CREATION.

"These Great and Mighty Beings work always directly for the Wondrous Godhead, which is the ABSOLUTE.

"They work unceasingly within the confines of the Great Law of Manifestation.

"Blessed are the Supreme Lords of Creation.

"There are no words in any language to express the Beauty of These Ones.

"There are no thoughts in any mind-belt, which could possibly do half-justice to the Wondrous Power of These Ones.

"For They are beyond description.

"They are beyond the true belief of even the adepts.

"They are beyond the comprehension of the Suns.

"There is the ONE in the Centre.

"There are the Seven Central Suns.

"There are the Ninety-one Galactic Lords.

"There are the nine hundred million Solar Logi.

"There are the countless trillions of Worlds—and all these have been brought into Wondrous Manifestation by the Supreme Lords of Creation, who work as The Seven—round The One.

"And yet They are above even this, for the Greater Part of These, paradoxically enough is not even in Manifestation.

"They are the Divisions in . . . . . Which is the Beginning.

"They are the Potential within . . . . . Which is the End.

"They are the Realisers of the Potential and the Potential—Itself.

"They are the Creators and Preservers of ALL Manifestation.

" These are the GODS—of the Gods !

" These dwell in the Highest Places in all the vast Universal System.

" These are Sacred beyond description.

" They are the Shining Ones.

" They are the Givers of Light.

" They are the Spirits of Flame.

" They are the Great and Mighty Energies, which course through each Galactic System.

" These Ones give Their Power so that all life may express itself in a million million different forms, in order to gain that experience which will take it—in full consciousness—back to its Source.

" These Great and Mighty Gods are behind even —THIS !

" Blessed are These Ones, throughout all Infinity, in the Timelessness of—NOW—in the unchangeability of Reality, which exists within the Heart of Hearts of—THE ABSOLUTE.

" These are Blessed throughout the NOW—in the NOW.

" SO ENDETH THE ELEVENTH BLESSING.

" Oh My sweet adorable children, send your Love to These Great and Mighty Ones, so that it may be returned to you by the Great Law. So that, when it is returned, freely can you dispense this Wondrous Power to all those around you.

" Oh children, send your Love. SEND YOUR LOVE.

" Oh children, take THAT which is given back unto you and even then give it unto others and it will be Recorded by the Hand of Truth, in the Timeless Book of Records—that you did this.

" And you will shine among men.

"You will be greater by far than a King. Stronger than an Emperor, as Wise as an Oracle, as Gentle as a Lamb—when you do this.

"Oh adorable little children, take these, My Texts—and read them well. Accept them as your Bible—and ACT upon these—and you will be of great service to your brothers.

"Oh Mighty, Wondrous Jehovah,
  Let the Light from Your Heart,
  Let the Love from Your Heart,
  Let the Power from Your Heart,
  Fall upon the heads of all these Earth children
  So that they may be made strong and
  Wise and capable of unselfish Love.
  So that they may be able—always—
  To render service to their brothers."

"Oh adorable children—GO WITH GOD."

—Delivered on Sunday, October 5th, 1958.

The Twelfth Blessing

SAINT GOO-LING

"NOW today Prasad will again be dispensed. (The Prasad was Blessed).

"Now then when Master Jesus asks for the Crosses, you will place them.

"He will then Bless them at His convenience. Then our good friend here (George King) after the Celebration, will hand out a Cross to each one personally, who will come up after and take the Cross.

"Do not let anybody else handle this, for once it has been given into your custody and you accept it, then that virtually becomes a symbol of your acceptance of these last great Teachings of Jesus.

"When you do this, you have responsibility of bearing witness to your fellow men of the words of Jesus, in these your times.

"Then you will be equipped to speak of these things you have learned.

"When you have learned them—with your hearts—then you can go forward and spread the Light of your Power and your enhanced knowledge of these Cosmic Teachings, to your brothers.

"For know this—these teachings are not given to you—but *through* you.

"Would like to offer most heartfelt thanks to all those who co-operated with these Twelve Blessings. To all you who came here—and especially to you dear people who sacrificed the Bliss of the Blessings to take active part in all forms of service which were necessary in order to guarantee the faithful continuance of this Operation—to you, dear friends, go my greatest thanks.

" It is unnecessary for me to offer thanks to the one who enabled these Blessings to be given to Earth, for he has read the Book—and has seen it there! But declaration has not yet quite dawned —but will do so !

"Now, during this Blessing, please, dear friends, sit very quietly and send your Power to the Focal Point—the One and Only Point.

" I go ! "

BLESSED IS THE ABSOLUTE

THE MASTER JESUS

" Oh My adorable children, where you gather in My name, truly, truly, there shall I be.

" Oh children, control your minds, control your emotions and walk through Silence—into— Silence. Then you will be one with the All-Knowledge Space which exists within each and every one of you.

" Then come ye outwards in service. For verily, do I say unto you, that the greatest one in these days is he who sacrifices himself—his bliss and the whole of his energy—for the benefit of his brother.

" This one is great. Be ye like this !

" Prepare yourselves, Oh adorable children. Give yourselves the ability to be of service—*and then be of service*—so that your brother may be helped through you.

" BLESSED IS THE ABSOLUTE.

" In all ITS Terrible Glory.

" In all ITS Silent Immobility.

"In all ITS Ever-moving Manifestation.

"In all ITS Silent—yet complete—Consciousness.

"Greater than all the Worlds is THIS—for IT contains them.

"Greater than all the Suns is THIS—for these are the Centres of ITS Wondrous Body.

"Greater than the Great Galactic Lords is THIS —for these are activated Centres of Preservation within this Mighty Frame.

"Greater than even the Seven Lords of Creation is THIS—for these are ITS Hearts.

"Greater than even the One within the Centre is THIS—for this is but ITS Brain.

"IT is above all these things. IT IS—all these things—and even more than THAT !

"BLESSED IS THE ABSOLUTE—IN ALL THE WONDROUS GLORY OF ITS MANIFESTATION.

"IN ALL THE UNCHANGEABILITY OF ITS REALITY.

"IN ALL THE COMPLETE IMMOBILITY OF ITS SILENT SELF.

"FOR THIS IS THE BEGINNING—AND THE END.

"AND IT IS THE STAGE BEFORE THE BEGINNING—AND THE STAGE AFTER THE END.

"THERE IS NOTHING IN ALL THE WORLDS OUTSIDE OF—THIS !

"FOR THIS IS—ALL IN ALL—AND ALL IN ALL—THAT !

"BLESSED IS THE ABSOLUTE.

"Not even the Supreme Lords of All Creation could do justice to the picturisation of the Magnificence of—THIS !

"For IT IS the Former of The Great Cause, which, coming before Potential—These Ones can use.

"IT is the—I AM—within man.

"IT is the—Life within all things.

"IT is the—rain.

"IT is the—drought.

"IT is the—gentle breeze of summertime.

"IT is the—mighty wind across the seas.

"IT is the—seas.

"IT is the—emptiness of Space.

"IT is the—fullness contained within Space.

"IT is the—Worlds.

"IT is ever—and Forever and FOREVER.

"IT IS INFINITY—and yet it is more than this—for IT IS behind even these things.

"This, Oh adorable children—IS THE GOD. THIS IS THE GOD which cannot ever be limited by man or God-man.

"THIS THING—THIS ALL THINGS—IS NOW BLESSED.

"SO ENDETH THE TWELFTH BLESSING.

"Oh little children, do not let the fools of your World limit your concept. Do not let them limit your thought. Do not let them limit your visualisation. Do not let them limit your Soul— but think upon these things. Let these Truths enter into your consciousness, so that—you may be better prepared for your journey through Experience.

"Bring unto Me now these Crosses.

(Here the 53 little wooden Crosses were placed upon the table before the Gentle Master. He then took a Cross from the tray on which they were standing and held it in His right hand, high above His head, so that all might see.)

" Look at this !

" Look what the Christian Church has done to it ! It is these people who have stained it with the continual flow of My Blood.

" This, My children, is *not* the symbol of death. It is the Symbol of Resurrection. It is not the Symbol of the terrible death depicted by your foolish priests ! It is the lasting Symbol of Resurrection of the Spirit of Man, up to the Mighty Godhead—through Karmic Experience. That is what it is !

" Because of such—it is a Holy Symbol.

" Treat it as such. Make it known that it is such !

" You will not be popular. If you take these, My Texts, into your World, you must be prepared to divorce yourself from popularity in this World —as yet.

" But just as I Resurrected after the crucifixion, so do I state now, that when you do this, you will live through the Mighty Triumph of *your* Resurrection.

" Let no man touch this one except he who now holds it.*

" These Symbols are Blessed, as the Symbols of Resurrection. They will hold that Power as long as this World does last. For even if you destroy them now, the Power will not leave them.

" **Oh Mighty Jehovah,**
Let the Wondrous Power from Your Everlasting Heart,
Fall upon the heads of all those upon the Earth—NOW.
Let the Wondrous Love from Your Mighty Heart,
Fall upon the hearts of all those upon the Earth—NOW.
So that they may all realise their
Divine heritage
And One-ness with THEE.

" Oh adorable children—GO WITH GOD."

* This reference was made to the Cross which had been held up as Jesus addressed His band of new Disciples.

THE INVOCATION

THE MASTER AETHERIUS

"So the Operation known as The Twelve Blessings is now over.

"Dear friends, you have been asked to go forward into your World to spread these Teachings. It is up to you to do this.

"Now, I would like to make this announcement.

"Owing to the para-normal strain upon Mental Channel No. 1, we will retain Transmission silence until Saturday next (October 18th, 1958).

"This person must rest in the meantime. He has been responsible for warding off terrible calamity from this Earth and therefore must take into due consideration the strain imposed during this Operation.

"Naturally, of course, every dark force was thrown against this one—but their efforts were not fruitful.

"Now, dear friends, before I vacate Transmission Orbit, I will give you the benefit of my Invocation.

" I Invoke the Power

From the Supreme Lords of Karma—NOW.

May this Power fall upon the heads

Of all Terrestrial people—NOW,

So that they may know that

God dwells silently within them all."

(Here The Great Master Aetherius intoned a most beautiful Chant in a language not known to this Earth.)

"Good evening, my dear friends."

—Delivered on Sunday, October 12th, 1958.

The Last Blessing

The Last Blessing was given by George King, Chairman and Founder of The Aetherius Society, during a Special Service held at the Headquarters in London on April 4th, 1959.

At this time, George King, seeming to be surrounded by a halo of great Light, delivered this simple yet beautiful and well-deserved Blessing to that Wondrous Being, Jesus, Who had made a great sacrifice upon the behalf of all men.

This Blessing has been included in this impression of The Twelve Blessings in answer to numerous requests.

Although The Twelve Blessings constitute a complete course of mystic practices, The Last Blessing, given as it was, by our Enlightened Leader, should be practised by all those who hold the Master Jesus in reverence.

BLESSED IS JESUS

" Oh Divine Spirit of all Creation, we send our love and our Blessings to the giver of The Blessings—The Master Jesus."

" This is the last Blessing.

" Blessed is He, Who in wonderful simplicity, came among us, to stay here upon this Earth and to die, so that man upon Earth might be given an opportunity to come that little bit nearer to the Heart of God.

" Blessed is Jesus.

" Thrice Blessed is the Body of Him.

" Seven times Blessed is the Heart of Him.

" Nine times Blessed is the Mind of Him.

" And once and always Blessed in the Heart of God is The Spirit of Him."

"Oh Mighty Brahma,
Divine Lord of Creation,
Send Forth the Power of Thy Love—NOW,
So that we might direct it to this
Wonderful Angel, Who walked in lonely yet
Shining simplicity among us.
Send it through us unto this One,
So that He might use this Energy to
Further His Great Mission upon this Planet
And upon any Planet He would visit.
Send forth Thy Power, Oh Brahma.
Allow us, Oh Brahma, to do this one little thing
In return for the Sacrifice made
By this Great Being.
It is done, even as we request, for it is written
That man's extremity is Thy opportunity.
For this, we bow our heads in eternal gratefulness,
To Thee and to Thy Disciple—JESUS,
Who is forever among us."

—Delivered on Sunday, April 4th, 1959.

CONCLUSION

After the Twelfth Blessing had been delivered by the Master Jesus, the fifty people who had attended most of these Transmissions came forward to receive their little Crosses, made Holy by the Blessing put upon them by Jesus.

Later, at Aetherius House, on October 18th, 1958, that great Orator and New Age Prophet, known to Earth simply as Mars Sector 6, in a speech emphasising the vital importance and the all-embracing significance of The Twelve Blessings, gave advice which is equally applicable to all those who read this book and accept the Truth of its content.

His following statements have been chosen as a fitting conclusion to the New Age Bible known as The Twelve Blessings.

Jesus has come again in this twentieth century to extend His Ancient Mission to save this Earth. It is now up to you, the New Disciples who read, learn and accept these Teachings, to take your rightful place as sowers of the seeds of Cosmic Truth throughout your World.

GO YE FORTH

"Oh brothers of Earth, during these past few weeks—in your time—the Master you knew as Jesus, has extended His Mission to Terra by giving the Teachings known as The Twelve Blessings.

"These Teachings were given by the Venusian you murdered.

"In these Teachings known as The Twelve

Blessings, this person you called Jesus, gave an enhanced concept of Reality, so that the men of Terra, in these days, could take these Teachings in the light of scientific knowledge—in the light of proposed Space travel—and broaden their minds accordingly.

" Think ye well upon these things !

" Go ye forth—in multitudinous ways—to spread this Word !

" For two thousand years the Christian Religion has hidden the Great Truths contained within its Holy Works. You unordained ones must—if you would be saviours of your Planet—put right this most terrible wrong by spreading the extended teachings of Jesus, with their simple—yet profound—Cosmic Concept.

" You notice, Oh Disciples, that these Teachings are not limited.

" Be ye like them !

" Limit not yourselves but—be unlimited. For verily do you take into your World a concept of the Infinite, Everlasting, Timeless Reality of the Mighty Absolute.

" Why be limited when your weapons of Wisdom be as broad as Timelessness—Itself ?

" Throw from your back limitation put there by the dictators of your policy.

" Rise, at this very moment into the Realms of Limitless Expansion and—GO YE FORTH ! "

MARS SECTOR 6.

OM SHANTI SHANTI SHANTI.